SOLAR ECLIPSE
Activity Book for Kids

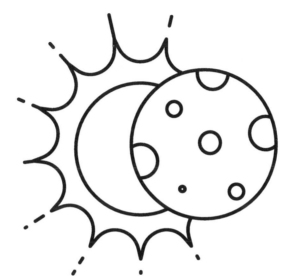

This book belongs to..

_____

_____

_____

Table of Contents

Hello, Super Space Explorers! 🚀✨

Guess what? Something super cool and special is about to happen in the sky! It's called a solar eclipse, and it's like a game of cosmic hide-and-seek where the Moon sneaks in front of the Sun, making it look like night-time during the day for just a little bit!

Are you ready to be an Eclipse Detective? 🌑🔍 You're going to learn all about this awesome event and have tons of fun with activities and games in this book. We're going to draw, solve puzzles, and even become space scientists together!

Get your space suits on (okay, maybe just your favorite t-shirt will do) and let's get ready for an adventure that's out of this world! 🌟

We're super excited that you're here. It's not every day we get to see the Moon cover up the Sun, so let's make it an adventure to remember!

Let's blast off and dive into the world of eclipses and all its wonders! 🚀📖

Wishing you the most stellar time, Your Eclipse Adventure Team

What is a Solar Eclipse?

Ever see a game of peek-a-boo with the sun and the moon? That's a solar eclipse!

Imagine the big, bright Sun is like a flashlight in the sky, and the Moon is a giant cookie that moves right in front of it. When this cookie covers the flashlight, it gets a bit dark for a little while—just like a quick night time during the day!

So, when the Sun, Moon, and Earth play this special game of lining up, we get to see the Moon's shadow on Earth, and that's the solar eclipse. It's super cool because it doesn't happen all the time. We have to wait for the perfect moment when everyone gets in a straight line.

Get your eclipse-watching gear ready! It's time to see the Moon play hide and seek with the Sun!

Solar System Trivia Blast!

Sun Questions

1. Question: What kind of gas makes up most of the Sun?

2. Question: Is the Sun a star or a planet?

3. Question: How many Earths could fit inside the Sun?

Moon Riddles

4. Question: Does the Moon have light of its own?

5. Question: Who was the first human to walk on the Moon?

6. Question: Why do we only see one side of the Moon from Earth?

Earth Puzzlers

7. Question: What is the name of the layer of air around the Earth?

8. Question: How long does it take for Earth to orbit all the way around the Sun?

9. Question: Do all planets have the right conditions for life as we know it?

Solar System Trivia Blast!

Eclipse Brain Teasers

10. Question: What happens to the sky during a total solar eclipse?

11. Question: How often do solar eclipses happen?

12. Question: Can looking at a solar eclipse without protection hurt your eyes?

Solar System Trivia Answers!

Sun Answers

1. Answer: The Sun is mostly made up of a gas called hydrogen!

2. Answer: The Sun is a star, the biggest and closest one to Earth!

3. Answer: About 1 million Earths could fit inside the Sun because it's so huge!

Moon Answers

4. Answer: No, the Moon reflects sunlight just like a giant mirror in space!

5. Answer: Neil Armstrong was the first to take steps on the Moon way back in 1969!

6. Answer: Because the Moon rotates once on its axis in the same time it takes to orbit the Earth. That's why we always see the same side!

Solar System Trivia Answers!

Earth Answers

7. Answer: It's called the atmosphere, and it's like Earth's cozy blanket!

8. Answer: It takes one year for Earth to make a full trip around the Sun.

9. Answer: As far as we know, Earth is the only planet in our solar system with the right conditions for life like plants, animals, and humans.

Eclipse Answers

10. Answer: During a total solar eclipse, the sky gets dark as if it's suddenly nighttime!

11. Answer: Solar eclipses happen about 2 to 5 times a year, but seeing a total solar eclipse from the same place on Earth can take many years!

12. Answer: Yes, looking at a solar eclipse without special glasses or a viewer can damage your eyes, so always use protection!

Remember, space cadets, each fact you learn makes you smarter and a better explorer of our amazing universe!

Solar Eclipses Through Time: A Historical Adventure

Gear up, young time travelers, because we're going on a trip way back in history to discover the amazing story of solar eclipses!

Long ago, before we understood what a solar eclipse really was, people all around the world came up with their own fantastic tales and explanations.

A Time of Myths and Legends

- **Hungry Dragons:** In ancient China, people believed a giant dragon was eating the Sun! Everyone would bang on drums and make loud noises to scare the dragon away and save the day.
- **The Sun and the Moon's Dance:** The ancient Greeks thought a solar eclipse happened when the Sun and the Moon met up for a secret dance in the sky, taking a break from lighting up the earth.
- **The Sleeping Sun:** The Native American Pomo tribe told a story of a bear who got into a tussle with the Sun and took a big bite out of it. After the eclipse, the Sun needed to rest and heal—kind of like a bedtime story for the sun!

Scientists Crack the Code

As years went by and people learned more about the stars and planets, they figured out the true story of eclipses.

- **Predicting Patterns:** A long, long time ago in ancient Babylon, smart astronomers started predicting when eclipses would happen by paying close attention to patterns in the sky.
- **Eclipse Explained:** Way back in the 1500s, a scientist named Johannes Kepler used math to explain that eclipses happen because the Moon casts a shadow on Earth.

Eclipses in History

Solar eclipses didn't just make people wonder—they also lined up with some pretty big moments in history!

- **Battle of the Eclipse:** In 585 BC, a solar eclipse suddenly darkened the sky during a big battle between two ancient armies. They were so surprised that they stopped fighting and decided peace was a better idea!
- **Einstein's Big Idea:** In 1919, a solar eclipse helped prove Albert Einstein's theory of relativity. When the Sun got blocked, stars' positions seemed to shift, just like he said they would because of gravity bending light. Whoa, science!

Solar eclipses have always been dazzling and mysterious, inspiring stories, songs, and discoveries. They remind us that there's always more to learn and that the universe is a wild and wonderful place.

Now, as eclipse detectives, we can enjoy these awesome events with our own eyes, and maybe even dream up new stories for future space explorers to tell!
 blocked, stars' positions seemed to shift, just like he said they would because of gravity bending light. Whoa, science!

Eclipse Countdown Calendar

21 Days Countdown

19 March	20 March	21 March	22 March
23 March	24 March	25 March	26 March
27 March	28 March	29 March	30 March
31 March	01 April	02 April	03 April
04 April	05 April	06 April	07 April

APRIL 08 ECLIPSE

Monday, April 8, 2024 Afternoon

Check NASA for location based time tables at: https://science.nasa.gov/eclipses/future-eclipses/eclipse-2024/where-when/

What time will you start your Eclipse party?

_____

_____

_____

_____

_____

_____

Cosmic Activity Countdown

With the amazing Solar Eclipse happening on April 8th, we've got a universe of cool activities planned just for you! Each day from now until the eclipse, you can dive into a new, fun activity right here in your very own Cosmic Activity Countdown!

Inside these pages, you might zigzag through mazes like you're dodging asteroids, hunt for hidden words like a space explorer, or color your way through a galaxy full of stars and planets!

So, grab your pencils and your astronaut imagination! It's time to start the countdown with a burst of fun every day until the solar eclipse wows us in the sky!

Are you ready, young explorers? Blast off into the world of activities and let the excitement rocket you all the way to eclipse day

Word Search - 1

Can you find all the words from the list below?

```
G  M  G  O  H  T  D  K  O  U  S  M
A  S  R  K  R  R  A  X  T  B  H  H
R  O  V  G  E  B  A  W  F  J  Z  R
T  L  D  T  C  N  I  F  N  E  K  A
O  A  J  S  L  I  M  T  M  M  K  L
T  R  Z  U  I  F  O  X  J  Z  Q  K
A  G  T  M  P  U  O  T  C  B  S  W
L  K  M  B  S  Q  N  X  P  Y  H  A
I  K  A  R  E  A  E  B  U  K  A  W
T  C  C  A  C  O  R  O  N  A  D  J
Y  F  S  U  N  B  E  A  M  H  O  G
M  C  E  L  E  S  T  I  A  L  W  U
```

CELESTIAL	CORONA
ECLIPSE	MOON
ORBIT	SHADOW
SOLAR	SUNBEAM
TOTALITY	UMBRA

18

Word Search - 2
Can you find all the words from the list below?

B	P	H	E	N	O	M	E	N	O	N	G
N	Y	P	X	M	O	W	A	T	G	E	Y
N	M	A	O	I	U	U	W	S	L	H	V
Q	R	T	V	W	O	L	X	C	R	E	D
V	V	H	X	H	Z	L	A	I	A	O	A
H	R	U	G	M	A	T	P	J	K	Y	R
Y	D	O	Z	I	C	V	K	X	K	C	K
I	C	V	T	E	J	B	H	S	A	Q	N
W	D	R	P	E	N	U	M	B	R	A	E
B	A	S	D	E	L	J	C	I	B	R	S
P	A	S	T	R	O	N	O	M	Y	G	S
S	O	L	A	R	I	Z	E	F	X	C	S

ASTRONOMY
PARTIAL
PENUMBRA
SKY
SPECTACLE

DARKNESS
PATH
PHENOMENON
SOLARIZE

Word Search - 3

Can you find all the words from the list below?

```
S  L  P  H  E  N  O  M  E  N  A  K
X  N  N  S  B  N  D  G  Y  D  C  X
T  I  I  L  U  X  H  Y  Y  V  T  P
W  G  G  G  G  N  H  D  H  P  T  L
I  H  H  Z  L  R  L  T  G  O  K  E
L  T  T  Z  A  O  N  I  P  F  Y  M
I  F  J  N  O  E  W  S  G  H  K  P
G  A  U  L  V  R  N  B  K  H  T  G
H  L  W  E  T  U  C  E  W  P  T  A
T  L  O  B  S  N  T  O  T  A  L  R
W  N  I  M  I  T  K  Q  L  P  H  Y
S  V  X  B  K  C  P  G  D  A  S  Y
```

EVENT	GLOW
LUNAR	NIGHT
NIGHTFALL	PHENOMENA
SUNLIGHT	SUNSPOT
TOTAL	TWILIGHT

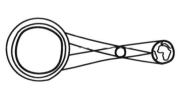

20

Word Search - 4

Can you find all the words from the list below?

```
X  I  F  O  B  S  C  U  R  E  B  E
G  A  O  H  L  Z  W  O  N  D  E  R
Q  F  I  M  T  E  D  J  D  K  E  A
Q  H  E  H  A  B  E  A  Y  N  K  L
P  T  G  C  Y  R  K  J  I  R  L  I
D  I  O  M  E  E  V  H  A  O  Y  G
S  X  D  H  O  B  S  E  R  M  X  N
C  J  P  N  C  O  Q  A  L  A  I  M
B  S  T  S  C  G  C  G  B  W  K  E
F  I  G  D  U  K  W  F  F  S  A  N
G  R  A  N  R  O  W  B  N  P  V  T
E  O  C  C  U  R  R  E  N  C  E  J
```

ALIGNMENT
OBSCURE
OCCURRENCE
SIGHT
WONDER

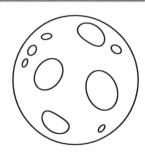

MARVEL
OCCUR
SHINE
SPHERE

Word Search - 5

Can you find all the words from the list below?

```
P  T  E  N  E  B  R  O  U  S  S  E
U  V  A  N  I  S  H  I  N  G  Z  D
X  G  O  C  C  U  L  T  B  F  O  T
R  N  S  E  M  R  H  H  J  L  I  H
A  Q  N  P  X  S  P  C  P  S  N  S
D  Q  J  U  N  U  I  V  N  T  Y  O
I  X  I  O  M  T  R  A  F  F  I  L
A  Z  C  Z  C  B  R  L  P  F  A  S
N  X  V  A  N  T  R  C  N  I  K  T
T  T  L  E  D  W  O  A  Z  Q  Q  I
G  A  D  E  R  F  N  F  L  L  W  C
G  P  H  E  N  O  M  E  N  A  L  E
```

GALACTIC
PHENOMENAL
SOLSTICE
TRANSIT
VANISHING

OCCULT
RADIANT
TENEBROUS
UMBRAL

22

Word Search - 6

Can you find all the words from the list below?

```
G  S  Y  H  T  H  V  E  E  J  U  J
W  P  G  M  E  Z  L  J  X  B  F  P
A  E  W  P  M  G  Q  Q  P  A  O  X
V  C  U  E  L  G  W  B  A  J  L  S
E  T  N  N  P  N  V  W  N  M  U  A
L  R  V  E  C  H  E  E  S  R  M  E
E  U  E  T  D  R  A  X  E  G  I  N
N  M  I  R  D  U  L  S  I  S  N  M
G  C  L  A  M  I  V  N  E  U  O  L
T  J  I  T  M  U  E  F  Z  S  U  I
H  R  N  E  T  X  R  Z  M  R  S  M
H  T  G  P  W  E  G  Q  H  C  B  J
```

ENIGMA
LUMINOUS
PHASES
UNVEILING

EXPANSE
PENETRATE
SPECTRUM
WAVELENGTH

Word Search - 7

Can you find all the words from the list below?

```
I  R  Z  T  A  D  V  M  X  N  I  N
S  L  E  W  R  P  N  I  F  D  K  D
E  C  L  S  Z  A  E  L  K  E  Y  A
L  O  Z  U  P  W  D  R  E  V  G  V
N  S  E  S  M  L  A  I  T  D  N  H
P  M  N  J  H  I  E  N  A  U  I  S
D  I  I  I  M  A  N  N  I  N  R  B
M  C  T  A  O  S  D  A  D  N  C  E
A  H  H  I  Y  A  F  O  T  E  G  E
P  S  T  E  L  L  A  R  W  I  N  A
O  V  R  S  T  W  S  H  A  Y  O  T
S  V  E  N  D  G  A  K  E  C  V  N
```

APERTURE
ILLUMINATION
RESPLENDENT
STELLAR
ZENITH

COSMIC
RADIANCE
SHADOWY
WANING

Sudoku - 1

Look at the 9×9 grid divided into nine 3×3 sub grids. Each row, column, and subgrid must contain all the numbers from 1 to 9 without repetition.

	8	5	7		3		9	
3	9	6				7		8
2		7	5	9	8	4		
7	6		8				4	
8		3			9	5	6	1
5		1	6		4		8	7
	5				7	6	1	4
6		8	4		5	3	2	
1		4	9		6		7	

Sudoku - 2

Look at the 9×9 grid divided into nine 3×3 sub grids. Each row, column, and subgrid must contain all the numbers from 1 to 9 without repetition.

	2	5	1		8	4		
7			3	6			8	1
8	1	3	2			6	5	7
		1	4		6		3	
4	9	2	8		7	1	6	5
	6		5			7	4	2
		4	6			9	7	
9		6	7	8				4
1	8	7	9		3	5	2	

Sudoku - 3

Look at the 9×9 grid divided into nine 3×3 sub grids. Each row, column, and subgrid must contain all the numbers from 1 to 9 without repetition.

	1	8	5	6	7	4	3	9
5		6			3	1	7	
9			2	4	1			
	9			5		7	8	3
	5					9	2	6
3			6	7		5		1
	6		7	2		3	1	5
1		3	8			2	6	
4		5	1	3		8	9	

Sudoku - 4

Look at the 9×9 grid divided into nine 3×3 sub grids. Each row, column, and subgrid must contain all the numbers from 1 to 9 without repetition.

3	5	4		2		1		8
		8	5		9	3	6	2
9		6	8	3		7	4	
	8			7	2			
	4			1	8		2	6
			6	5		9	8	7
4	1		2	8		6	3	
8						2	5	4
	6	2	4	9		8	7	1

Connect the dots and color the image

Connect the dots and color the image

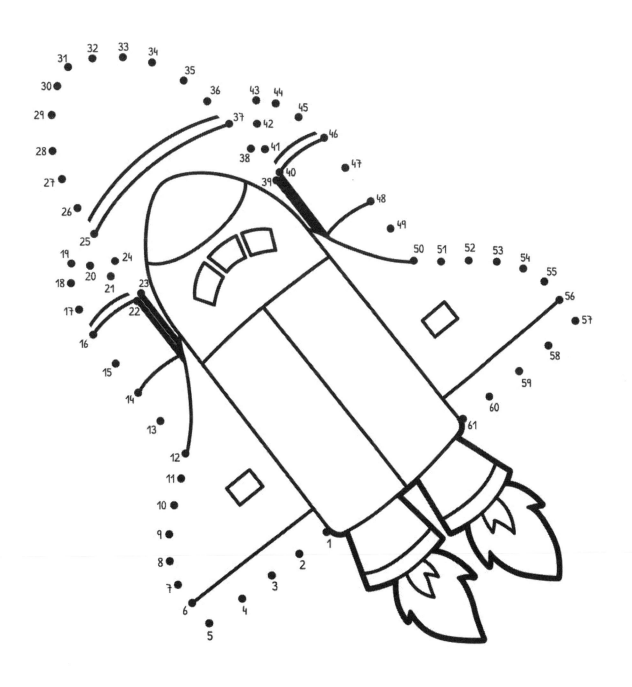

Connect the dots and color the image

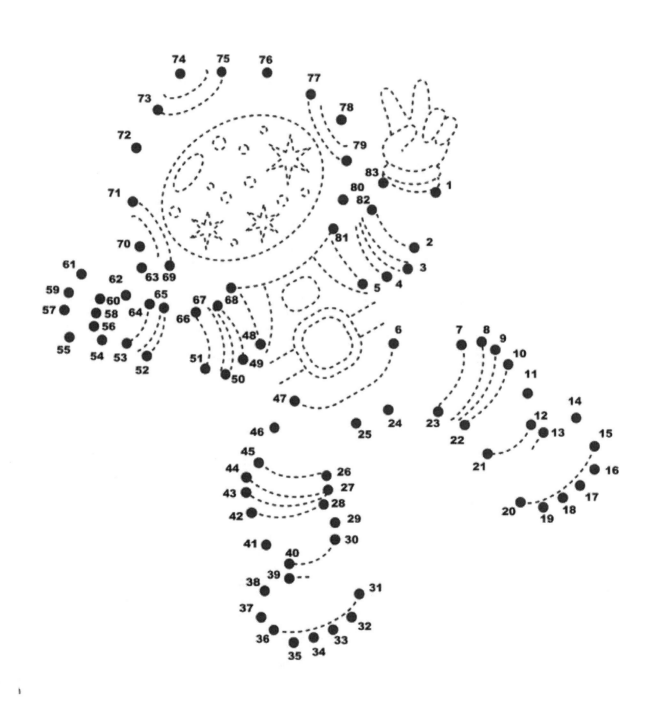

Tic Tac Toe

Tic Tac Toe

Tic Tac Toe

Word Scramble - 1

Rearrange the following words to create new words, using all the letters in the original word. These words are called anagrams.

cpeisle   = _____

owshda   = _____

bmeausn   = _____

omno   = _____

umrba   = _____

nraoco   = _____

oayitttl   = _____

borit   = _____

elsetiac   = _____

oslar   = _____

Word Scramble - 2

Rearrange the following words to create new words, using all the letters in the original word. These words are called anagrams.

denasrs = _____

ptha = _____

rtosyomna = _____

nphenemoo = _____

colutnactoi = _____

olraszie = _____

mnuarepb = _____

ysk = _____

apltira = _____

etcleaces = _____

Word Scramble - 3

Rearrange the following words to create new words, using all the letters in the original word. These words are called anagrams.

igtnfhall = _____

uontssp = _____

wolg = _____

raunl = _____

glhtiwti = _____

vnete = _____

rtstian = _____

amlnigen = _____

peerhs = _____

enshi = _____

Word Scramble - 4

Rearrange the following words to create new words, using all the letters in the original word. These words are called anagrams.

maatcrslino = _____

ccuro = _____

rboescu = _____

ihts = _____

arlmev = _____

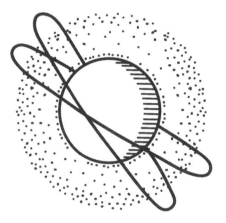

deornw = _____

cltgaaic = _____

hzienit = _____

ilalnutinoim = _____

dneplsantre = _____

Word Scramble - 5

Rearrange the following words to create new words, using all the letters in the original word. These words are called anagrams.

wnnagi = _____

rsyeecrode = _____

tiixqsue = _____

ruseyiot = _____

rcpetasl = _____

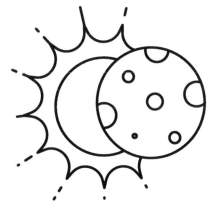

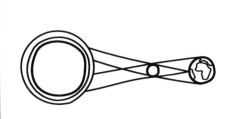

canera = _____

ghtilninme = _____

panelt = _____

anhnvsgi = _____

giaezn = _____

Maze - 1

Take a moment to look at the entire maze layout and identify key features like dead ends, open paths, and the entrance/exit points:

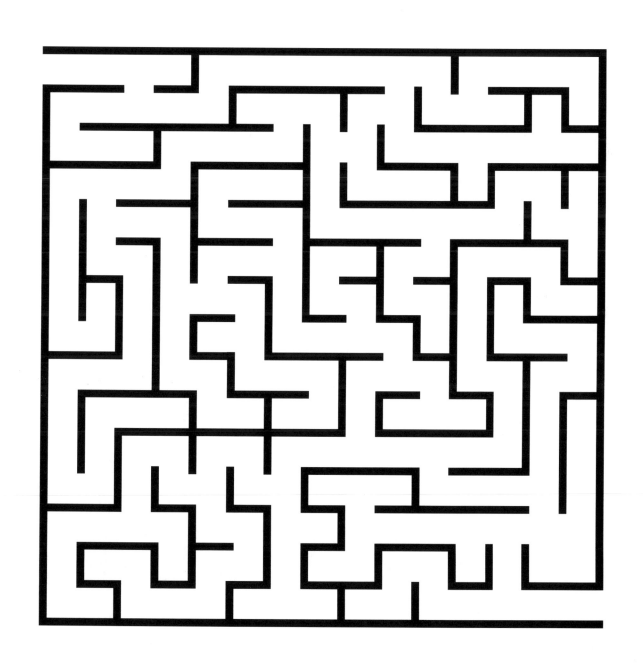

Maze - 2

Take a moment to look at the entire maze layout and identify key features like dead ends, open paths, and the entrance/exit points:

Maze - 3

Take a moment to look at the entire maze layout and identify key features like dead ends, open paths, and the entrance/exit points:

Timeline of the Eclipse

Are you ready for a once-in-a-lifetime sky show on April 8th, 2024? Grab your calendar, because you won't want to miss a moment of the Great Solar Eclipse! Here's the special timeline for this magical day:

Eclipse Party Time!

- **First Bite**: This is when the Moon takes its very first tiny nibble out of the Sun. You'll see a small chunk of the Sun go 'poof'—it's starting!

- **Moon Munch**: As the Moon moves more in front of the Sun, it looks like it's munching away, getting bigger and bigger until it almost covers the whole Sun!

- **Totality Awesome**: This is the big moment! The Moon completely covers the Sun and it gets really dark for a couple of minutes. Stars might even pop out and say hello!

- **Sun Smiles Again**: After "Totality Awesome", the Sun will start to peek out bit by bit, just like a shiny crescent moon.

- **Moon Waves Goodbye**: The Moon says bye-bye to the Sun as it moves away completely, and the Sun shines bright like it normally does.

Best Spots for Eclipse-Watching!

- Texas: Howdy, partner! In Texas, the eclipse starts early and you'll see a lot of it!
- Midwest Magic: In places like Illinois and Indiana, get your picnic blankets out for a fantastic view.
- Hello, Northeast: If you're in New York or Maine, you'll get a special ticket to the eclipse show.

Even if you're not in the spots mentioned for the best eclipse view, you can still enjoy the show!

The solar eclipse will be visible in many places across the world, just in different ways:

- **Partial Peek:** If you're not on the path where the eclipse is totally covering the Sun, you'll still see it as a partial eclipse. The Moon will cover a part of the Sun and it will look like a special cookie with a bite taken out of it!
- **Live Streams:** You can watch the eclipse live on TV or online! There will be lots of places to see the eclipse in action, right from your screen.
- **Eclipse Events:** Many local museums, science centers, and astronomy clubs will have eclipse parties with special telescopes to watch safely.

You may share in the excitement from wherever you are! Just remember, never look at the Sun without special eclipse glasses or proper protection, because the Sun is super bright and can be a big owie for your eyes.

So get set for a day of sky-watching adventure, and let's count down to the eclipse together!

Eclipse Reflections

Grab your pencil, markers, or crayons—it's time to be an Eclipse Artist and Reporter! After you've watched the amazing solar eclipse, let's put your thoughts and feelings on paper. Here are some fun questions to get you started:

Draw the Moment!

1. Can you draw a picture of what the solar eclipse looked like? Was the Moon completely covering the Sun or just a bit?

2. Can you draw a picture of what the solar eclipse looked like? Was the Moon completely covering the Sun or just a bit?

Your Eclipse Story

3. How did you feel when you saw the eclipse? Were you excited, surprised, or did it make you think of a space adventure?

_____

_____

_____

_____

4. Write down the story of your eclipse day. Who were you with, and what did you do to prepare for the big moment?

_____

_____

_____

_____

_____

Science Thoughts

5. What's one cool fact you learned about the Sun, the Moon, or the Earth from this eclipse?

_____

_____

_____

_____

_____

6. If you were a scientist studying the eclipse, what would you like to find out?

_____

_____

_____

_____

Future Eclipses

7. Would you like to see another eclipse? Where would be your dream place to watch it from?

_____
_____
_____
_____
_____

8. If you could share this eclipse with anyone in the world or anyone from history, who would it be and why?

_____
_____
_____
_____
_____

Share and Compare

9. Now that you've drawn and written your eclipse experience, share it with your friends or family. What did they think and feel?

_____
_____
_____
_____

10. Compare your eclipse artwork and stories. What's similar, and what's super unique about each one?

_____

_____

_____

_____

_____

Remember, every eclipse is a new chance to look up, wonder, and learn. Keep exploring, keep drawing, and keep asking questions—the sky's not the limit, it's just the beginning!

More Celestial Wonders in 2024!

After the spectacular solar eclipse, mark your calendars because the sky's got a lot more to show you this year!

■ Perseid Meteor Shower: August 11-12

Imagine the sky lighting up with shooting stars—it's the Perseid Meteor Shower! Find a dark spot, lay back, and watch the sky sparkle. Remember, it takes a bit for your eyes to play "I spy," so give 'em time, and you'll see the stars play hide-and-seek!

✺ **Orionid Meteor Shower:** September 26 - November 22

Make a wish upon a shooting star... or maybe twenty! The Orionid Meteor Shower is here with a meteor dance-off. Stay up late and keep your eyes on the sky—the best things come to those who wait!

● **Partial Lunar Eclipse:** September 18

Watch the Moon put on a red hat during the Partial Lunar Eclipse. Without any glasses, you can see the Earth's shadow make the Moon blush. It's the perfect night to moon-gaze with your family!

🔭 **Saturn at Opposition:** September 8

Saturn's in the spotlight, shining super bright. With a little help from a telescope, you might see Saturn's rings like shiny hula-hoops around it. Wave hello to Saturn—it's showing off just for you!

Get Set, Junior Astronomers!

Charge up your twinkle tracker goggles (your eyes!) for these super-cool space parties. Look up, and whisper to the sky, "Show me something amazing!" Chances are, it'll twinkle back at you with a meteor or a sparkly planet!

WORD SEARCH SOLUTIONS

Word Search Solutions

Puzzle #1 - Solution

```
G M G O H T D K O U S M
A   S R K R R A X T B H H
R   O R V G E B A W F J Z R
T L A D T C N I F N E K A
O O A J S L I F O X J Z Q K
T L R Z U M O N T M M K L
A A G T M P U T C B S W
L R K M B S Q N X P Y H A
I   I K A R E A E B U K A D W
T   C C A C O R O N A D J
Y   F S U N B E A M H O G
M C E L E S T I A L W U
```

Puzzle #2 - Solution

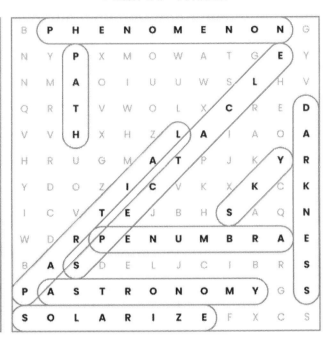

```
B P H E N O M E N O N G
N Y   P X M O W A T G E Y
N M   A O I U U W S L H V
Q R   T V W O L X C R E D
V F   H X H Z L A I A O A R
H R U G M A T P J K Y K
Y D O Z I C V X X K C N
I C V T E J S A Q N
W D R P E N U M B R A E
B A S D E L J C I B R S
P A S T R O N O M Y G
S O L A R I Z E F X C S
```

Puzzle #3 - Solution

```
S L P H E N O M E N A K
X   N N S B N D G Y D C X
T I I L U X H Y Y V T P
W G G G G N H D H P T L
I H H L R L T G O K E
L T T Z A O N I P F Y M
I F J N O E W S G H K P
G A U L V R N B K H T G
H L W E T U C E W P T A
T L O B S N T O T A L R
W N I M I T K Q L P H Y
S V X B K C P G D A S Y
```

Puzzle #4 - Solution

```
X I F O B S C U R E B E
G A O H L Z W O N D E R
Q F I M T E D J D K E A
Q H E H A B E A Y N K L
P T G C Y R K J R L I
D I O M E V H A O Y M
S X D H O B S E R M X E
C J P N C O Q A L A I
B S T S C G C G B W K N
F I G D U K W F S A T
G R A N R O W B N P V T
E O C C U R R E N C E J
```

53

Word Search Solutions

Puzzle #5 – Solution

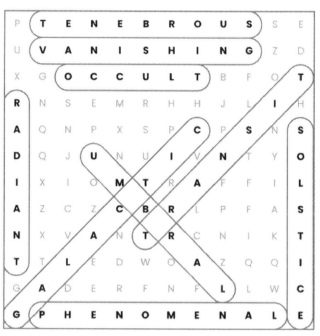

Puzzle #6 – Solution

Puzzle #7 – Solution

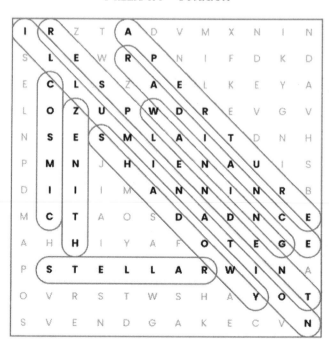

SUDOKU SOLUTIONS

Solution 1

4	8	5	7	6	3	1	9	2
3	9	6	1	4	2	7	5	8
2	1	7	5	9	8	4	3	6
7	6	9	8	5	1	2	4	3
8	4	3	2	7	9	5	6	1
5	2	1	6	3	4	9	8	7
9	5	2	3	8	7	6	1	4
6	7	8	4	1	5	3	2	9
1	3	4	9	2	6	8	7	5

Solution 2

6	2	5	1	7	8	4	9	3
7	4	9	3	6	5	2	8	1
8	1	3	2	9	4	6	5	7
5	7	1	4	2	6	8	3	9
4	9	2	8	3	7	1	6	5
3	6	8	5	1	9	7	4	2
2	3	4	6	5	1	9	7	8
9	5	6	7	8	2	3	1	4
1	8	7	9	4	3	5	2	6

Solution 3

2	1	8	5	6	7	4	3	9
5	4	6	9	8	3	1	7	2
9	3	7	2	4	1	6	5	8
6	9	1	4	5	2	7	8	3
7	5	4	3	1	8	9	2	6
3	8	2	6	7	9	5	4	1
8	6	9	7	2	4	3	1	5
1	7	3	8	9	5	2	6	4
4	2	5	1	3	6	8	9	7

Solution 4

3	5	4	7	2	6	1	9	8
1	7	8	5	4	9	3	6	2
9	2	6	8	3	1	7	4	5
6	8	5	9	7	2	4	1	3
7	4	9	3	1	8	5	2	6
2	3	1	6	5	4	9	8	7
4	1	7	2	8	5	6	3	9
8	9	3	1	6	7	2	5	4
5	6	2	4	9	3	8	7	1

WORD SCRAMBLE SOLUTIONS

Word Scramble - 1

Eclipse	Corona
Shadow	Totality
Sunbeam	Orbit
Moon	Celestial
Umbra	Solar

Word Scramble - 2

Darkness	Solarize
Path	Penumbra
Astronomy	Sky
Phenomenon	Partial
Occultation	Spectacle

Word Scramble - 3

Nightfall	Event
Sunspot	Transit
Glow	Alignment
Lunar	Sphere
Twilight	Shine

Word Scramble - 4

Astronomical	Wonder
Occur	Galactic
Obscure	Zenith
Sight	Illumination
Marvel	Resplendent

Word Scramble - 5

Waning	Arcane
Transparency	Illumininght
Exquisite	planet
Mysterious	Vanishing
Spectral	Enigma

Made in the USA
Las Vegas, NV
05 April 2024